EARLY MUSIC SERIES 12

CONTINUO PLAYING
ACCORDING TO
HANDEL

EARLY MUSIC SERIES

CONTINUO PLAYING ACCORDING TO HANDEL

His figured bass exercises

With a commentary by
DAVID LEDBETTER

CLARENDON PRESS · OXFORD
1990

Oxford University Press, Walton Street, Oxford OX2 6DP
Oxford New York Toronto
Delhi Bombay Calcutta Madras Karachi
Petaling Jaya Singapore Hong Kong Tokyo
Nairobi Dar es Salaam Cape Town
Melbourne Auckland
and associated companies in
Berlin Ibadan

Oxford is a trade mark of Oxford University Press

Published in the United States
by Oxford University Press, New York

British Library Cataloguing in Publication Data
Handel, George Frideric, 1685–1759
Continuo playing according to Handel: his figured bass
exercises.—(Early music series; 12).
1. Continuo playing
I. Title II. Ledbetter, David III. Series
781.47
ISBN 0–19–318434–6
ISBN 0–19–318433–8 (pbk.)

Library of Congress Cataloging in Publication Data
Handel, George Frideric, 1685–1759.
Continuo playing according to Handel.
(Early music series; 12)
1. Thorough bass. I. Ledbetter, David. II. Title
III. Series: Early music series (London, England: 1976); 12.
MT49.H35 1989   89–751031
ISBN 0–19–318434–6
ISBN 0–19–318433–8 (pbk.)

Typeset by Moonye
Printed in Great Britain by
Bookcraft (Bath) Ltd

CONTENTS

INTRODUCTION

Nobody who has acquired the ability to accompany baroque music from a figured bass will be satisfied to return to using written-out realizations. Apart from the fact that accompanying from figures is one of the most rewarding of musical experiences, it has immense practical advantages. By having the bass in direct proximity to the solo line(s) on the page, the continuo player feels in the closest contact with the parts accompanied. With an editorial realization there is an intervening stave (which most experienced players will in any case want to ignore) putting the bass at one remove from the other parts. The feeling of contact is further enhanced by the layout of original sources, where figures are normally placed over rather than under the bass with the result that the player's eye has a significantly smaller area of the page to take in. But the main advantage is in fact one of the reasons why the system of bass figuring was originally devised — it allows flexibility in the choice of accompanying instrument, and the same part can be used for organ, harpsichord, lute, or theorbo, each of which has its own accompanimental style. The texture and tessitura of the accompaniment can also be adjusted to suit the instrument accompanied. In the many baroque sonatas which allow alternative instrumentation the accompaniment will not be the same for the quiet flute or recorder as it is for the more extrovert oboe or violin. On a more mundane level, it is in fact easier to accompany from figures (when the facility has been acquired), since the player can adapt the accompaniment to his own hand and technique. What is required is often a great deal simpler than that which many written-out accompaniments provide.

With the general availability of original sources in facsimile, there is no longer any excuse for neglecting this essential musical skill. But of the many seventeenth- and eighteenth-century tutors which describe chords and basic progressions, very few offer exercises which inspire the musical imagination or take the student in an orderly way from the simplest to the most elaborate type of realization. Fortunately there exists an exceptionally fine set of exercises by Handel which amply fulfil both these requirements. Handel's style has a characteristic solidity and sonority which, because it is so familiar to us, constantly suggests idiomatic ways of realizing these exercises. They also reveal that he was, when the occasion arose, an inspired teacher.

Handel devised the exercises between 1724 and the mid-1730s, when he was harpsichord teacher to the Princesses Anne, Caroline, Amelia, and Louisa, daughters of George II. Princess Anne, the Princess Royal, was unusually gifted and a lifelong friend of the composer, who clearly thought it worth taking the trouble to devise a comprehensive course for her. The figured bass exercises form only part of a complete composition tutor which ranges from the most basic note-against-note exercises to examples of fugue and canon. A full account of the origin, sources, and structure of the tutor, together with facsimiles, is given by Alfred Mann in a supplementary volume of the *Hallische Händel-Ausgabe* (see Suggestions for Further Reading). The figured bass exercises are of two types.

1. *Exercises in figured bass*

These are ordered in an unorthodox but very logical way. Handel's approach is an entirely practical one, based on chord shapes and figures rather than on the concept of root-position chords and their inversions. Thus the $\frac{6}{5}$ chord, the first inversion of a seventh chord, comes early in the exercises (No. 12) where it follows naturally the $^6_4$ chord introduced in No. 11, and precedes the seventh chord in root position in No. 16. Each exercise introduces a new chord, or a new use of a chord, and neatly consolidates material already covered. The set's great merit is that, as well as giving the basic chords and the most common progressions involving them, it weaves these together in a musical way. The materials of baroque harmony may broadly be reduced to two elements — scale sequences and cadence formulas. Whereas other tutors give these in abstract fragments, Handel in each case demonstrates the possibilities of a given progression in a logical way and provides complete pieces of musical character which are gratifying to play.

2. *Exercises in fugue*

Improvising a fugue may initially seem a daunting exercise. We tend to think of a fugue as something intellectually conceived and carefully worked out on paper, needing time and patience to perfect its details. This is because we are most familiar with one tradition of baroque fugal writing where the fugue is obbligato in all its parts, i.e. it is in a set number of independent parts and capable of being written in open score (as were many fugal works for keyboard, from the Fantasias of Frescobaldi to Bach's *Art of Fugue*) and of being performed, in theory at least, on melody instruments.

Handel's exercises relate to another tradition, that of the improvised fugue. Here the fugue hardly has a set texture, still less a fixed form, but is more an effect. Its only distinguishing feature is that there should be a principal subject which enters successively at different pitch levels. Integrity of parts is not necessarily maintained, and connecting material is made up from what are essentially elaborations of basic continuo formulas. Handel's own keyboard fugues are written-out examples of this tradition, as are the fugue-type sonatas of Domenico Scarlatti.

These are just the sort of exercises with which the young Handel would have begun his study of fugue with his teacher Zachau. The approach is purely practical, the processes are quite clear, and there is nothing arid or intimidating about them. They are excellent practice for continuo players, in that they are designed to cultivate a sense of line and an ability to think in independent parts rather than merely to follow the mechanical habits of the hands.

The commentaries on individual exercises are designed to give only the essential information needed for their interpretation. I have tried to keep them as brief as possible, although those on the earlier exercises are necessarily longer since they define basic principles. Since examples can give information more clearly and concisely than words, I have included specimen realizations for all of the exercises in an appendix. These are no more than my own humble suggestions, but I hope that they may clarify many individual points and be a useful model against which students can check their results.

Assertions made in the commentaries are based on the consensus of a wide range of seventeenth- and eighteenth-century treatises. It would be cumbersome and unhelpful to give references for all of these in what is intended as a basic tutor. I have included brief notes on the most helpful treatises in the Suggestions for Further Reading, and players are strongly encouraged to explore these.

The complexities of figured bass notation will be much simplified if it is borne in mind that there are only nine basic figurings: 6 and $^6_4$ for the first and second inversions of triads; 7, $^6_5$, $^4_3$, and 2 for seventh chords and their inversions; and 4–3, 7–6, and 9–8, for the three types of suspension. Most of the rest are extensions of these when accidentals are required. There are also a few figures for appoggiatura chords or chords over a pedal which are more complex. In the commentaries, I have referred to chord factors entirely in terms of figured bass numerals. It would be extremely confusing to mix these with the numerals used in traditional harmony textbooks to denote the function of notes in a chord.

Pitches are referred to by means of the Helmholtz system as shown here.

c   c′   c″

EXERCISES IN FIGURED BASS

Root-position triads

No. 1

This first exercise is designed for practising the three most common bass progressions using root-position chords: progressions by fourths and fifths (bb. 1–3, 6–7); by falling thirds (bb. 3–4); and by rising seconds (bb. 4–5, b. 6).

In order to get maximum benefit from the exercise, you should keep strictly to the traditional disciplines of elementary figured bass playing. There are three basic principles.

1. Play one note in the left hand (LH) and three in the right (RH). The RH notes are the octave, fifth, and third above the bass.
2. Move to the nearest available position of the next chord. The essence of fluency in figured bass playing is that you should be equally familiar with all the possible RH shapes of each chord. Thus the first chord has three possible shapes, depending on whether the octave, third, or fifth is on top (Ex. 1). The shape you use for the succeeding RH chord will depend on your

Ex. 1

point of departure. You will notice that different bass intervals require different numbers of notes to be changed in the RH. If the bass moves a third, only one RH note will need to be changed; if the bass moves a step, all three RH notes will need to be changed. If you are playing these exercises on an organ, you should tie any common notes between chords.

3. When the bass moves by step (bb. 4–5, b. 6) the RH parts *must* move in contrary motion to it. This avoids the parallel fifths and octaves which would result from similar motion between upper parts and bass, and is the main exception to the principle of moving to the nearest available position of the next chord. Seventeenth- and eighteenth-century tutors are strict about parallels, and they should certainly be avoided in basic exercises.

To begin with, play No. 1 three times keeping to these principles. Start with the octave on top of the first chord, then with the third, and then with the fifth.

Whilst playing the exercise in this way is useful for acquiring fluency in moving from one RH chord shape to the next, it does give a rather mechanical result. In order to get a better structured melodic line, two further aspects of style should be taken into account.

1. Where there is a sequence in the bass, have a corresponding sequence in the RH. The first three bars have a sequence of rising fifths and a fourth. In order to get a corresponding RH sequence, begin with the same factor on top in bb. 2 and 3 as in b. 1, and move to the nearest available position for the second chord of each bar. The rest of the exercise should be played in accordance with the basic principles, i.e. moving to the nearest available RH position for the falling thirds in bb. 3–4 and bb. 5–6, and using contrary motion for the steps in bb. 4–5 and b. 6.

2. At a cadence, when the RH chord has the root of the dominant as the top note of the penultimate chord, it is dull to repeat this note as the fifth on top of the final tonic chord. Drop down a position to have the third on top instead.

These principles of style will improve the melodic profile of the top part and give it a natural relationship to the shape of the bass line. Such a basic exercise gives little scope for imaginative melodic realization, but it is excellently designed to cultivate the basic reflexes which must be natural in good continuo playing.

No. 2

When the bass moves in crotchets, there need not be a change of chord from one note to the next in every case. The most obvious example of two bass notes having the same chord is where the bass leaps an octave (bb. 1 and 5). There will thus be some variety in the rate of chord change, and it is important that this harmonic rhythm is reflected in the RH. There is no need to repeat the RH chord on the second crotchet beat of b. 1 or the last of b. 5. Otherwise, the basic principles remain in operation. First play the exercise with the root on top, then try with the third and the fifth.

b. 1. Have a minim RH chord for the first two beats. For the falling thirds in the second half of the bar, move to the nearest available position of the next chord.

bb. 1–2. The step across the barline requires contrary motion.

bb. 2–3. A sequence of rising fourths begins on the second beat of b. 2: use a corresponding RH sequence, with the same factor on top of the first of each pair of bass notes.

bb. 3–5. The last beat of b. 3 begins a sequence of rising fifths. Again, have a corresponding RH sequence. In both bb. 2–3 and 3–5 avoid having the same note on top of each pair (which gives a very dull effect). Thus, if you have *b'* on top of the second chord of b. 2, move down a position to have *g'* on top of the third chord, and so on down the sequence. Similarly, it is better not to have *e''* on top of the last chord of b. 3, which would give repeated top notes up the rising fifth sequence.

No. 3

Quavers in the bass line give scope for further variety in its rhythmic relationship with the RH chords. Usually one RH chord will last for four quavers, the fundamental harmony notes of the bass being decorated with passing notes, auxiliary notes, or other factors of the same chord.

bb. 1–3. The first of each group of four quavers is the basic harmony note, so the RH will play minim chords using the same principles of chord connection as in Nos. 1 and 2.

bb. 3–4. The harmonic rhythm increases from minim to crotchet beats in the second half of b. 3, giving the opportunity to use a very common method of harmonizing a rising scale known in the eighteenth century as the 'rule of the octave'. In its basic form, this alternates root-position (5) and first-inversion (6) chords as shown in Ex. 2. It should be played with two parts only in the RH (rather than three). The bass in bb. 3–4 of No. 3 is a decoration of this formula, and should be realized in either of two ways shown in Ex. 3.

Ex. 2

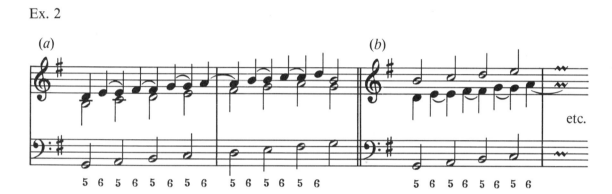

Ex. 3

No. 4

This is the first exercise in triple time, and also introduces the first 'figure' (a sharp) in its most usual context — as the leading note in a minor key. Accidentals on their own apply to the third of the chord. This exercise also demonstrates the two most common harmonic rhythms in triple time — one chord per bar (b. 1, bb. 4–8), and two chords per bar, where the chord change is on the third beat (bb. 2–3).

Use a sequence in the RH to mirror the sequence in the bass at bb. 2–4. In bb. 4–5 the bass falls a third, so keep to the nearest available position in the RH. In bb. 5–7 the rising fourth followed by a step should have contrary motion in the RH. The bass octave at b. 7 requires no change or repetition in the RH chord.

No. 5

The most common rhythmic subtleties of triple time are explored in this exercise. The harmonic rhythm has two chords per bar, and for most of the exercise (bb. 1–4) the chord change is on the third beat. In b. 5, however, the chord will need to change on the second beat, and the last three bars form a cadential hemiola (i.e. the speed of the triple time is halved). The rhythm of bb. 5–8 is therefore

Most of the decorative crotchets in the bass are passing notes, but some are chord factors other than the octave, such as the fifth in b. 2 (second crotchet) and the third in b. 2 (sixth crotchet). In bb. 1, 3, and 6 (first and second beats) and b. 5 (second and third beats) the bass runs from the root to the third of the chord. Many composers, particularly Italians, did not take the trouble to figure such obvious inversions, and neither did Handel. One might add at this stage that it is most satisfactory melodically if the RH has the octave on top of the final chord of a main phrase, particularly at the end of a piece.

No. 6

The sense of this exercise may not be immediately apparent from the figures. Its purpose is to introduce the remaining accidentals (flats and naturals). It is also an example of the simplest type of chromaticism — changing thirds. The exercise is cleverly arranged according to the principle of contrary motion between the hands so that the third is in a different part in each chord. In the sequence of rising fifths (bb. 1–2), with the thirds changing from major to minor, it is best to start in a fairly high position so that the RH can descend (Ex. 4a). Similarly, with the falling fifths (changing from minor to major, bb. 4–6) the RH parts will rise (Ex. 4b).

Ex. 4

6 chords

No. 7

This and the following two exercises demonstrate one of the most common uses of the 6 (i.e. $\frac{6}{3}$) chord — to harmonize ascending and descending scales. Traditionally there is only one way of playing these scales: with two parts only in the RH, the sixth on top and the third in the middle (Ex. 5). This gives parallel fourths between the top parts, which are acceptable. The alternative position (with the third on top) will give objectionable parallel fifths between the upper parts. A good way of using this exercise would be to restrict yourself to two parts in the RH throughout (except perhaps for the first and last chords), whilst trying to keep as many complete triads as possible.

The placing of the RH chords should reflect the harmonic rhythm — there is no need to change the chord when the bass leaps an octave (b. 1, first beat) or leaps a third down from a 6 chord (b. 1, second beat). The *f♯* in b. 2 (third beat) is an auxiliary note and should not be harmonized.

Ex. 5

No. 8

In minor keys, the sixth will sometimes need to be sharpened when it is a leading note. Conventions for notating this varied somewhat — German composers generally put a stroke through a sharpened 6 (6̸), as here. The 5 in b. 4 (first beat) will also need to be sharpened, and similarly has a stroke through it (5⁺).

The texture in this exercise could well be varied, using three notes in the RH for root-position chords or for 6 chords which are not in sequence (as in b. 2). As a general rule, when playing three notes in the RH for a 6 chord it is best to double the bass note, except when the bass is a leading note, in which case you should double the sixth.

The best RH position at the opening is with the octave (*e″*) on top since the next note will have to be *d♯″* according to the rule for playing parallel 6 chords (see Ex. 5).

Off-beat quavers which are passing notes (b. 2, second and sixth quavers; b. 3, second quaver; and b. 4, fourth quaver) or harmony notes (b. 2, fourth and eighth quavers) do not require a chord change.

No. 9

This final exercise for 6 chords gives the remaining chromatic inflexions (6♭ and 6♮) and combines 6 chords with altered thirds (6̸♭). It is best to begin with the fifth on top, since the first chord is followed by a scale sequence. The rising chromatic sequence at b. 5 will be stronger if played with three parts in the RH.

Suspension of the third (4–3)

No. 10

This exercise introduces the most common suspension and one of the simplest forms of dissonance. The full figuring for the 4 chord is $\frac{8}{5}$, and the three possible RH positions for this chord are shown in Ex. 6.

Ex. 6

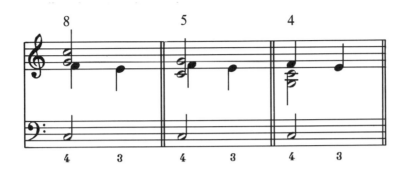

In No. 10 bb. 1–4 are intended to harmonize a descending scale in the uppermost part, so the RH should begin with *f″* on top. In this scale the three possible RH shapes for the 4–3 will alternate.

In bb. 6 and 8 the 4–3 suspension appears in its most usual context, as a decoration of a perfect cadence. At b. 6 the major third of the dominant is indicated by a natural, at b. 8 by a sharp.

Many of the subsequent exercises have a plain form of a progression at their openings and a version of the same progression with a decorated bass line later in the piece. In this exercise the progression from the second half of b. 11 is the same as at the opening and likewise should begin with *f″* on top, descending through a scale of F major to the end of the exercise.

$\frac{6}{4}$ chords

No. 11

The $\frac{6}{4}$ is the most common type of double suspension or appoggiatura (other types will be seen in Nos. 20–1). In most instances in this exercise it will not be necessary to change the RH chord at the $\frac{6}{4}$, since it is the same as the chord before. Thus in b. 1 the $\frac{6}{4}$ is a chord of B flat, resolving as a $\frac{5}{3}$ chord of F major on the fourth beat.

Since bb. 1–3 have a sequence in the bass, the RH should use a corresponding one. If the RH begins with *d″* on top (the most effective position), b. 2 will begin with *e♭″*, and b. 3 with *g″*. From the second half of b. 3 the RH will descend, using the three possible positions of the $\frac{6}{4}$ shown in Ex. 7.

Ex. 7

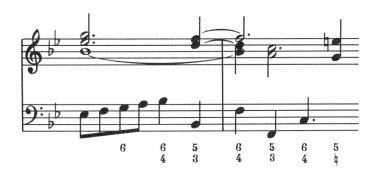

With more decorated bass lines such as that in this exercise, care should be taken to make the RH reflect the underlying harmonic rhythm. The added parts should form clear and logical progressions. Fussy elaboration will only weaken the final effect.

$\frac{6}{5}$ chords

No. 12

In this exercise Handel introduces the most important scale sequence of baroque music after the 'rule of the octave' (see No. 3) — the circle of fifths. This has three basic forms:

1. with root position seventh chords (7, see No. 16);
2. with first inversion seventh chords ($\frac{6}{5}$);
3. with third inversion seventh chords (2, see No. 14).

Handel's logic is practical, rather than pedantically literal, in giving the sequence first in its $\frac{6}{5}$ form, since it neatly follows on from the double figure ($\frac{6}{4}$) of No. 11.

Ex. 8

(*a*)

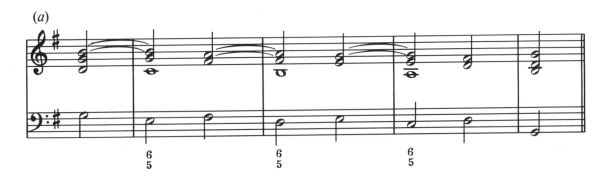

(*b*)

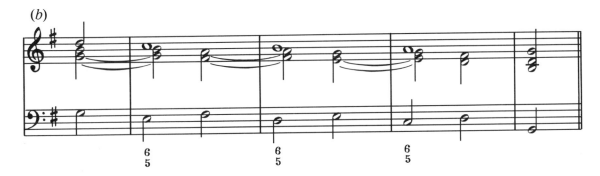

The $\frac{6}{5}$ chord has three possible RH shapes, as shown in Ex. 8. A close spacing (Ex. 8*c*) will yield stronger dissonances than an open one (Ex. 8*a*). When accompanying, the expressive context may well dictate which shape to use. This exercise is designed to alternate shapes, whether between sequences (bb. 1–2, cf. bb. 3–4) or in a cadence formula (bb. 9–10, etc.). It also has a repetition of the opening sequence, with a decorated bass, from b. 12.

At bb. 7, 12, etc., the same harmony over two crotchet beats is an opportunity to transfer the RH chord to a higher position in order to begin another descending sequence.

At b. 8 (third crotchet), and elsewhere in these exercises, Handel has placed the inflexion of the third as the top figure (i.e. $\frac{\flat}{6}{5}$, not $\frac{6}{5}{\flat}$). This may or may not have an implication for the layout of the chord, and composers were by no means consistent in this respect. Handel's figures are presented here as they appear in the source.

2 chords

No. 13

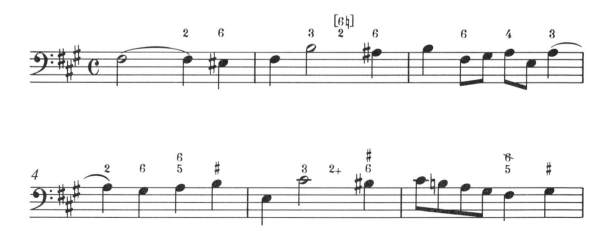

Ex. 9 shows the three common chords involving the figure 2: $\frac{5}{2}$, $\frac{5}{4}$, and $\frac{6}{4}$. The figure 2 on its own, however, almost invariably means the $\frac{6}{4}$. It is most commonly found over a suspended tonic note or over a suspended subdominant note. Normally the most effective position for this chord is with the 4 in the top part (as in Ex. 9c), but two other positions are possible and in this exercise it would be more stylish to have a different position in b. 2 from that used in b. 1.

The second figure in b. 5 is a 2 with a stroke (2+), indicating a sharpened second.

Ex. 9

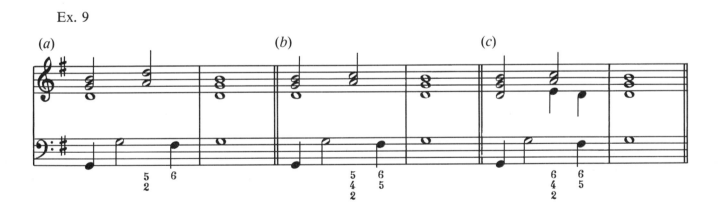

No. 14

The first five bars of this exercise give further practice for the 2 chord over tonic and subdominant notes, but now in a major key. Its main purpose is to introduce the version of the circle of fifths progression which uses third inversion seventh chords (see the note on No. 12). The complete progression in four parts is given in Ex. 10. It can also be played in three parts, omitting the tenor line of this example. Handel has used the full $\frac{6}{4}$ figuring here (as opposed to just the 2 in No. 13), presumably because he intended the sequence to be practised using the full four-part texture.

Ex. 10

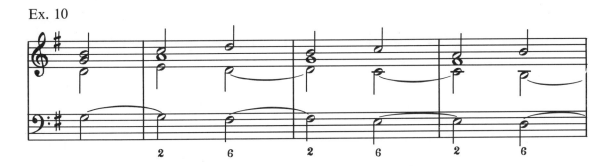

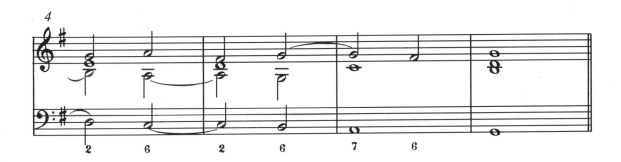

Suspension of the sixth (7–6)

No. 15

Exercises 15 and 16 introduce the figure 7. This has two uses: as part of a 7–6 suspension (No. 15) and as a root-position seventh chord (No. 16).

The 7–6 suspension is commonly used to decorate a cadence in which the tonic note in the bass is approached by step from above (No. 15, b. 5). It is also used in the descending version of the 'rule of the octave' scale (cf. the ascending version in No. 2, Ex. 2). Being in essence the decoration of a chain of parallel 6 chords, it should be played with only two parts in the RH (cf. No. 7, Ex. 5). There are two possible positions, which are shown in Ex. 11.

Ex. 11

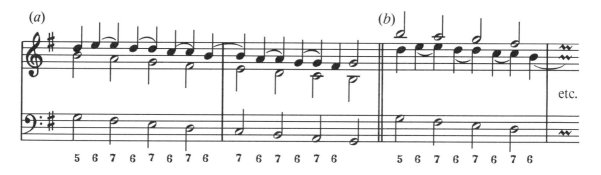

In this exercise one could well use the first position from b. 2, and the second from b. 6. From b. 8 the bass decoration could be imitated in the 7–6 resolutions.

7 chords

No. 16

Handel reserves the root-position version of the circle of fifths progression for this point in the exercises so that he can demonstrate the two basic uses of the figure 7 side by side. When accompanying, the texture of the RH chords will depend on the speed of the piece and the expressive context. A full five-part texture could be used in a slow tempo (Ex. 12*a*), four parts in a moderate tempo (Ex. 12*b*), and only the essential three parts in a quick tempo (Ex. 12*c*). In this exercise it is best to use the most fluent version (Ex. 12*c*).

Ex. 12

Suspension of the octave (9–8)

No. 17

Suspension of the octave, the last of the three suspension types, is often used in conjunction with the 4–3 to decorate the scale sequence shown in Ex. 13*a*. In bb. 2–4 and 8–11 of the exercise it is best to have the suspensions in the top part, since they are the most interesting aspect of the harmony and the descending scales which they yield are the most logical melodic lines.

As with seventh chords, spacing is an important consideration in the expressive use of the ninth chord. In a minor chord, if the third and the ninth of the chord are a major seventh apart in the RH the effect will be blander than if they are more closely spaced at a minor second, which gives a particularly acute dissonance. Some sleight of hand with the parts may be necessary to ensure a close spacing of the particularly expressive ninths at bb. 6 and 7.

The ninth should generally be at least a real ninth above the bass, i.e. producing the effect of a 9–8, not a 2–1. It is therefore advisable, as with other dissonances, to begin a sequence with the RH in a fairly high position, leaving it room to descend without getting too close to the bass. Again, some sleight of hand with the RH parts may be necessary to achieve this (see, for instance, the second beat of b. 8 as realized in the Appendix).

On the harpsichord, the player may well wish to savour particularly expressive ninths (as at bb. 6 and 7) by re-striking rather than suspending them.

Ex. 13

(a)

(b)

4 3 9 8 4 3   9 8 4 3 6 5

No. 18

Another common use of the 9 figuring is in the attractive cadence formula on which this exercise is based. Handel has used it in a sequence to harmonize a descending scale of E flat. Begin with *e♭″* in the top part, descending to reach *e♭′* on the third beat of b. 4.

Like other exercises, this one is in two sections and the bass line of the second is a decoration of the progression presented plainly at the beginning. The realization in bb. 11–14 can be exactly as in bb. 1–4.

For the B flat scale beginning at b. 7, one could well use an alternative trio sonata texture with only two parts in the RH and the suspensions in the inner part (see Ex. 14).

Ex. 14

No. 19

Based on a similar cadence formula to No. 18, this exercise gives an opportunity to experiment with expressive spacings of the ninth chord in a dark-hued minor key. A close spacing of the ninth and the third in the B flat minor chord at b. 6 has a particularly poignant effect, and could well contrast with an open spacing of the same chord at b. 7.

This exercise also gives scope for a rising melodic line, as shown in Ex. 15. The RH parts in this pattern are not strictly correct contrapuntally, since the ninth is not prepared in the same part as it is resolved, but such sleight of hand is very much part of the continuo player's art and in this instance the effective spacing of expressive chords is more important than contrapuntal correctness. Such dissonances are also best re-struck, rather than suspended, on the harpsichord.

In bb. 9–10 Handel gives a very characteristic and rich version of the II V I cadence formula, with a $\frac{6}{5}$ chord on both the sixth and seventh degrees of the scale. The RH should move in contrary motion to the bass here, using two different shapes for the $\frac{6}{5}$ chord.

From b. 9 to b. 12 the figures present another harmonization of a descending scale in the top part, which should begin on *d''*. This can be prepared as the top note of the last chord of b. 8.

Ex. 15

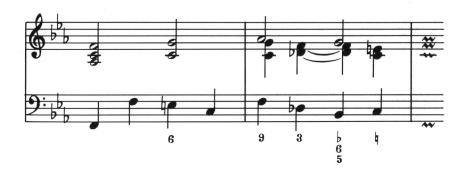

Double suspensions ($\frac{6}{4}$, $\frac{9}{4}$, $\frac{9}{7}$)

No. 20

Exercises 20 and 21 are for practising some of the richest and most expressive effects in baroque harmony. Of the three types of double suspension, the $\frac{9}{7}$ is the most colourful. (Full figurings for these chords are $\frac{8}{6}$, $\frac{9}{5}$, and $\frac{9}{7}$). As with other dissonances, spacing is of crucial importance to the expressive value of the chord; in deciding on a chord position the expressive context should always be taken into account. Compare, for instance, the effects of close and open spacings of the $\frac{9}{7}$ at the opening of the Sarabande from J. S. Bach's A minor English Suite (Ex. 16).

Ex. 16   J. S. Bach

In this exercise the $\frac{9}{7}$ chords are over bass notes which descend by step, and the RH will use the same position of the chord in sequence. One might well vary the RH positions by using an open spacing (starting with *d''* in the top part) from b. 2, and a close spacing (starting with *a'* on top) from the third beat of b. 6.

In order to gain fluency in changing from one position of this chord to another, practise Ex. 17 in which the three positions alternate. Start with the RH fairly high (*e''* on top) so that it has room to descend. At b. 4 you will need to transfer the RH up again. Use the repeated E minor chord to do this, with *g''* on top in the third beat.

Ex. 17

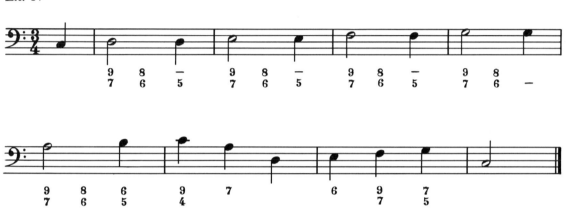

No. 21

Of the two other types of double suspension the $\frac{6}{4}$ is the blander and the $\frac{9}{4}$ slightly more colourful. Note the arrangement of these dissonances in the F minor Prelude from the second book of Bach's *Well-tempered Clavier* (Ex. 18). No. 21 alternates the $\frac{6}{4}$ and $\frac{9}{4}$ in a scale sequence similar to that in Ex. 13*b* (see No. 17).

Ex. 19 presents an exercise (similar to that given in Ex. 17) for practising the three RH shapes of the $\frac{9}{4}$ in alternation. Start with *e″* on top, and transfer the RH up to a position with *g″* on top at the third beat of b. 4. For a sublime use of these basic scale formulas, see bb. 29–39 and 71–83 of the six-part Ricercar from Bach's *Musical Offering*. This combines descending upper parts with double suspensions and a chromatically decorated version of the rising bass scale pattern demonstrated in No. 3, Ex. 2.

Ex. 18

J. S. Bach

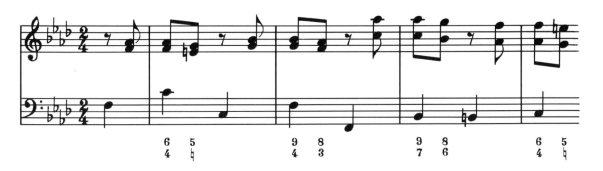

Ex. 19

Practice pieces

No. 22

Nos. 22–4 are extended pieces similar in intent to the 'Probestücke' of Mattheson's *Große Generalbaß-schule* (1731). The character and liveliness of the pieces derives from rhythmic decoration of basic progressions already presented in the exercises, and other than the pedal effects of No. 22, no new progressions are introduced.

The most common pedal effect is of a dominant chord over a tonic note. There are four variants of the dominant chord (see Ex. 20), and of these Handel uses only the $\frac{7}{4}{2}$ in this exercise.

Ex. 20

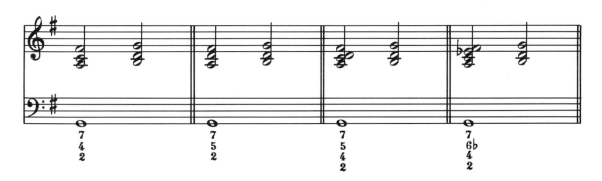

For a dominant pedal Handel gives a formula that is particularly common in the *galant* style and which involves two upper parts in thirds walking up and down a dominant seventh chord as shown in Ex. 21. In four parts the bass note is doubled (No. 22, bb. 4–6, 12–13, etc.).

Ex. 21

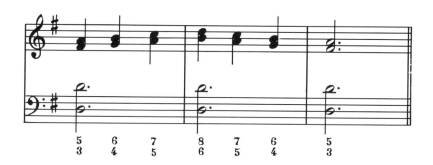

Ex. 22 shows the basic outline of a tonic pedal much favoured by Bach. The rich effect of a leading-note (usually diminished) seventh chord ($\begin{smallmatrix}7\\6\\4\\2\end{smallmatrix}$) over a tonic pedal may be extended to have a leading-note seventh chord resolving on to any degree of the scale. Reading the somewhat daunting figures which result from this is much simplified by the principle that any figure implying an augmented second ($\begin{smallmatrix}3\sharp\\2\flat\end{smallmatrix}$, $\begin{smallmatrix}5\sharp\\4\natural\end{smallmatrix}$, $\begin{smallmatrix}8\sharp\\7\natural\end{smallmatrix}$, etc.) normally means a diminished seventh chord. Since this is one of the most readily grasped shapes on the keyboard, it is necessary to read only one of the figures; e.g. 4♯ over a D will indicate a diminished seventh shape with a G♯ in it. These and other pedal effects are demonstrated in Ex. 23, an exercise which is freely adapted from the final pedal of Contrapunctus I from Bach's *The Art of Fugue*. A good practice piece for complex pedal effects is the opening chorus of the *St John Passion*.

Ex. 22

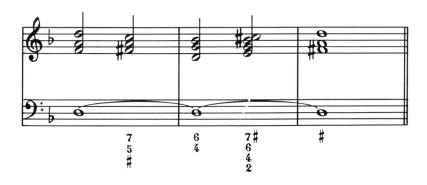

Ex. 23

b. 1. This is the first use of the second ($\frac{4}{3}$) inversion of a seventh chord. It is commonly used when the bass steps out the first three notes of a scale, with a top part moving in tenths with it (see Ex. 24). The parallel fifths between the top two parts have always been considered acceptable here.

Ex. 24

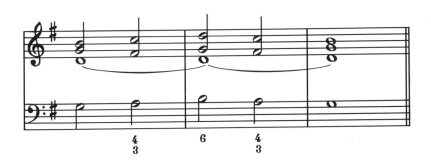

bb. 8–9. The hemiola should be made clear by means of phrasing and by tying the common notes between the last chord of b. 8 and the first of b. 9.

bb. 13, 17, etc. The rhythm implied by the figures is ♩ ♫ ♩

No. 23

Nothing very elaborate is required in the RH here. The decorative interest is in the bass, and the accompaniment needs strong harmonic definition only. The C clefs in this exercise and the next are as in the original, and familiarity with these is essential for a continuo player.

b. 7. The sequence of seventh chords here will have two parts only in the RH at this tempo.

bb. 9 ff. This needs some rhythmic pattern in the RH – minim chords would be very dull. As a general principle, it is much more effective to alternate two patterns rather than to repeat the same one. Compare the effect of the alternatives in Ex. 25, (*a*) with one pattern, (*b*) with an alternation of two.

Ex. 25

b. 13 ff. This pedal effect has a top part moving in tenths and sixths with the bass, as shown in Ex. 26.

Ex. 26

No. 24

In spite of the brilliant effect of this piece, most of the RH part can be made up of plain three-part chords connected according to the principles outlined in the basic exercises. However, the vivacity of the opening motif might well be enhanced by a RH figuration such as that suggested in Ex. 27, and using this for each entry of the main motif would also help to articulate the structure of the piece.

Ex. 27

The pattern at b. 16 etc. is similar to that in No. 23, b. 13 etc., and is realized in Ex. 28.

Ex. 28

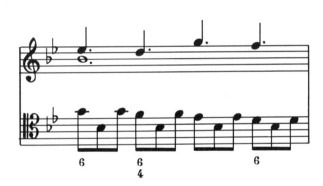

EXERCISES IN FUGUE

No. 1

This first exercise in fugue demonstrates the fact that baroque counterpoint is essentially the decoration of basic chord progressions, in this case the descending scale with 7–6 suspensions (see No. 15, Ex. 11). It should be realized in three parts only (except perhaps for the final chord, which could have four parts). The pattern for decorating the 7–6 suspensions given in bb. 6–8 should be continued in the later bars, though it could well be used in the alternative spacing given in No. 15, Ex. 11*b*, with the seventh in the inner part.

Specimen realizations for the exercises in fugue are given in the appendix, p. 96.

No. 2

Although this is the plainest of the fugue exercises, it is also the only one which keeps strictly to four parts. In Handel's shorthand notation of entries, the letters s, A, and T indicate the voice in which the subject enters. The pitch at which it enters is shown by symbols derived from German keyboard tablature (Ex. 29), which uses basically the same system as the Helmholtz pitch classification given in the introduction.

Ex. 29

The tenor and soprano answers are tonal, i.e. the interval *g–d* in bb. 1–2 will be answered by *d'–g* in bb. 2–3 and *d''–g'* in bb. 4–5. The principle behind this is simply that if the fifth of the tonic scale appears near the beginning of the subject, it is normally answered by the fourth of the dominant scale. This ensures that the opening of the fugue stays clearly in the tonic key.

Contrapuntal rigour is relaxed in the second half of b. 5, and the rest of the exercise can be realized in normal continuo style.

No. 3

Model

For Nos. 3, 5, and 6 Handel provided fully-worked model fugues as well as exercises, to demonstrate new and more elaborate procedures.

The preceding exercise was of the simplest possible type, with only one entry in each part followed by a chordal progression to bring the fugue to an end in the tonic. In No. 3 and its model the design is extended by having two entries in each part (in the model the second series of entries begins at the second half of b. 6). Variety is achieved by reversing the keys of subject (initially in the tonic) and answer (initially on the dominant), giving the following key scheme of entries:

voice	S	A	T	B	:	S	A	T	B
key	F	C	F	C	:	C	F	C	F
bar	1	2	4	5		6	8	9	11

This also neatly solves the problem that in a four-voice fugue the final entry of the exposition will normally be on the dominant, and is a common procedure known as fugal inversion. The fact that two successive entries are on C in this scheme (bass, b. 5; soprano, b. 6) accounts for the telescoping of the bass entry at bb. 5–6.

As well as this formal extension, Handel's model demonstrates the textures of improvised fugue and how these may be used to articulate structure. Most of the fugue is in three parts only, with rests to give emphasis to a new entry of the subject. A full four-part texture is reserved to give a sense of climax to the final bass entry (b. 11), to which the RH adds the usual continuo-style chordal suspensions. For the player, this may at first sight seem more complex and difficult than No. 2, but the apparent complications derive only from rhythmic decoration.

The exercise employs the same formal scheme as the model, but with a different sequence of entries:

voice	T	A	S	B	:	A	S	T	B
bar	1	2	3	4		8	9	11	13

Since the subject begins on the fifth degree of the scale, the alto answer at b. 2 will need to be tonal, in the form given by the bass at b. 5.

    Much of this fugue is concerned with various harmonizations for the quaver scale segment in the second half of b. 1. It will be in thirds with the given part in the first half of b. 3, and in sixths in the second half of b. 4 and the first half of b. 6. A three-part texture will be sufficient for most of the piece, except for the linking passage in b. 7 and the final bass entry from b. 13, which should both have continuo-style three-part chords in the RH. The final cadence could well be decorated with motifs from the subject.

No. 4

This takes up the subject of the model for No. 3 and adds two new features to a similar formal scheme. The first is a countersubject in invertible counterpoint with the subject (i.e. either may serve as a bass, although the possibility of inversion is not explored here). The second is the addition of a further set of entries (from b. 23) which extend the tonal range to the relative minor and, by abbreviating the sequential tail of the subject, create a climactic effect by having entries at ever closer rhythmic intervals. The form of the subject at bb. 23, 25, and 26 will in fact be identical to that of the model for No. 3. Thus the scheme of the fugue is as follows:

voice	S A T B	: S A T B	: A S T B
key	G D G D	: D G D G	: e a D G
bar	1 3 6 8	12 16 18 22	23 25 26 28

The given countersubject (from the second half of b. 3) will not be usable in precisely this form at every entry of the subject. But the effect of a regular countersubject can be produced by using its opening quaver leaps, which preserve rhythmic impetus through the subject's dotted crotchet opening.

No. 5

Model

A more rigorous exercise is Handel's preferred genre of double fugue, where both subject (**S**) and countersubject (**CS**) appear together at the first entry.

In the model, contrapuntal features which have been adumbrated in No. 4 are now given more systematic treatment. The invertible counterpoint of subject and countersubject is fully explored, and provides the main material of the fugue. The progressive decrease of the rhythmic interval between entries is now worked into a more developed stretto effect — the alto entry of the countersubject at b. 9 is followed by a soprano entry of the subject and tenor entry of the countersubject at b. 10. From b. 12 in the alto there is a sequential development of one of the countersubject motifs. This is preceded by the dotted crotchet–quaver of the beginning of the subject, which is immediately taken up by an entry of the subject proper in the bass. It is small rhythmic touches such as this which give good baroque counterpoint its felicitous effect. As Handel demonstrates, it is sufficient for the effect of a stretto if earlier entries follow a subject's opening notes with free figurations necessary to the harmony when the next voice with the subject enters, provided that the last entry in the stretto has the complete subject.

Another rhythmic ingenuity is the augmentation of the head of the subject in the tenor at b. 16. This prefigures the exploration of strict augmentation and diminution which provides the material for No. 6.

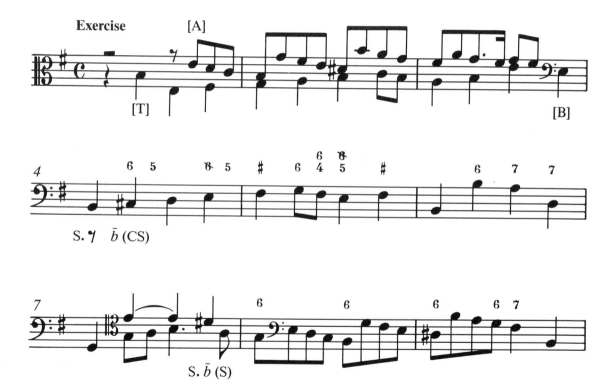

Of the devices used in the model, only that of invertible counterpoint appears in its compan-
ion exercise. But this model shows that even in a double fugue the texture need not be in more
than three parts except for the subject's final entry, where it fills out to four. It may even reduce
to two parts (model, bb. 7–8; exercise, b. 15). In spite of its contrapuntal elaboration, the exercise
is very playable since the subject and countersubject are designed to lie easily under one hand.
Free parts do not introduce complications — the tenor continuation from b. 4 can move mainly
in tenths with the bass.

From the end of b. 13 both subject and countersubject are in the upper parts.

No. 6

Sketch

Handel originally intended to conclude these exercises with demonstrations of the techniques of augmentation and diminution. Although the countersubject in the model for this exercise could be seen as a kind of free diminution of the subject, the piece as it was finally worked out hardly demonstrates these particular devices. Its place here can only be understood in the light of the preliminary sketch shown above (see Mann, *Theory and Practice*, pp. 17–18), in which the continuation of the subject appears in augmentation in the tenor from b. 6 (second minim).

The model does, however, demonstrate the effect of a denser texture. This is the result of a more compact subject than that in the model for No. 5, and one with a countersubject closely related to it rather than designed to contrast with it. In this it provides a fitting introduction to the extreme of thematic integration represented by No. 6. In fact, integration rather than contrast is the principle demonstrated in this model — the weaving of a harmonic fabric from a restricted number of motifs, a technique developed by Italian trio sonata composers of the mid-seventeenth century and most fully exploited by Purcell and J. S. Bach.

After the exposition of the invertible counterpoint in bb. 1–3, the alternative possibility of the countersubject being the leading voice is explored from bb. 4–6. At bb. 6–8 this concludes with a restatement of the countersubject in its original form in the dominant, and at the same time a new quaver motif (a rising fourth followed by descending steps) is introduced in the soprano (b. 7). This is of course related in outline to the subject. In bb. 9–11 a series of entries of the countersubject in the bass gradually link it to this motif. The organic integration of countersubject with subject (via the motif) is finally achieved in the soprano at b. 12, and its implications are fully spelt out in the final extended bass entry in b. 18.

Exercise

For the final exercise, Handel has a brilliantly effective *tour de force* — a double fugue in which the countersubject is a diminution of the subject. The execution of this is not nearly as difficult as it might at first seem, since only bb. 3–4, 7–9, and 12–13 require contrapuntal realization. The rest is either already realized or requires only decorated continuo chords.

bb. 3–4. Because of the pitch distance between subject and countersubject, a full four-part realization is required here. The RH will play what are essentially three-part continuo chords over the bass, with the subject in the top line.

bb. 7–8. The countersubject is in stretto in the upper parts. From the second beat of b. 7 the texture will consist of two parts only. When the soprano enters in b. 8 the alto will not be able to continue with the countersubject, and need only have harmony notes.

bb. 11–13. For the final stretto in the tenor and soprano, beginning at the last beat of b. 11, the subject can be virtually complete in both parts.

NOTE ON FIGURING STYLES

The degree of detail included in continuo figuring depends largely on the complexity of the music and the circumstances for which it was written. Italian composers, amongst whom one may include Handel, very often did not take the trouble to figure bass lines at all. Generally they wrote in a lucid and straightforward style for immediate performance, and the chordal accompaniment could safely be left to an experienced player (perhaps the composer) thoroughly versed in the harmonic formulas of baroque music. Figures, where given, are often incomplete and such matters as accidentals are generally left to the musicality of the performer. Only in music prepared for publication, such as the works of Corelli, was figuring systematically provided. German composers tended to be much more thorough in notating their intentions. This is particularly so in the case of J. S. Bach, who developed one of the most complex figuring styles partly because the accompaniments were generally intended to be realized by his pupils. French composers also evolved elaborate figuring styles: they published much more than the Italians and, as well as having a predilection for richly dissonant effects, they liked to include much 'instructive' detail in their notation. The figuring in François Couperin's chamber music is so detailed that, allowing for the conventions of the style and the tessitura of the solo instruments, the performer often has little choice as to what to play.

   The principal difference between French and German figuring conventions is in the notation of sharpened and flattened notes. German composers put a stroke through a sharpened note (6, 5^+, $4+$, $2+$), whereas the French used the stroke for the opposite purpose of indicating a diminished interval ($\not5$, $\not7$). The following useful instruction from Delair's *Traité* (1690) explains the French convention for the figure $\not5$: 'The flattened (or diminished) fifth, called the false fifth, takes the third and the sixth when the bass rises by a semitone (Ex. 30, x); in all

Ex. 30

Denis Delair

other cases it takes the third and the octave (y, z).' This is to say that $\cancel{5}$ means $\overset{6}{\underset{3}{5}}$ when on a lead-ing note which rises a semitone, and $\overset{8}{\underset{3}{5}}$ when it is part of a circle of fifths progression. Delair's instruction is not quite complete, since the bass often moves to the root of the dominant chord before rising a semitone from the leading note. In this case $\cancel{5}$ will also mean $\overset{6}{\underset{3}{5}}$, as shown in Ex. 31.

Ex. 31

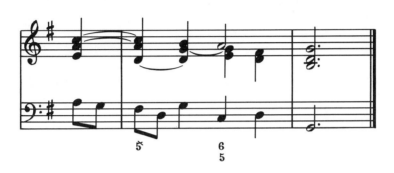

SUGGESTIONS FOR FURTHER READING

HANDEL

Mann, Alfred, *Georg Friedrich Händel: Composition Lessons from the Autograph Collection in the Fitzwilliam Museum, Cambridge* (*Hallische Händel-Ausgabe*, Supplement, Vol. 1), (Kassel: Bärenreiter, 1978).

___ *Theory and Practice: The Great Composer as Student and Teacher* (New York and London: Norton, 1987).

___ 'Handel's Successor: Notes on John Christopher Smith the younger', *Music in Eighteenth-century England: Essays in Memory of Charles Cudworth*, ed. C. Hogwood and R. Luckett (Cambridge: Cambridge University Press, 1983), pp. 135–45.

___'Bach and Handel as Teachers of Thorough Bass', *Bach, Handel, Scarlatti: Tercentenary Essays*, ed. P. Williams (Cambridge: Cambridge University Press, 1985), pp. 245–57.

The *Hallische Händel-Ausgabe* supplement gives a full account (with facsimiles) of the origins, sources, and structure of Handel's exercises. A concise summary of the main points, together with transcriptions of all the exercises, can be found in *Theory and Practice*. The essay on J. C. Smith has further information about their origin and a discussion (with facsimiles) of another autograph source for some of them. The tercentenary essay is a very illuminating comparison of the teaching methods of Handel and Bach.

TUTORS BEFORE 1800

Bach, Carl Philipp Emanuel, *Versuch über die wahre Art das Clavier zu spielen: Zweyter Theil* (Berlin: [author], 1762). Translated by W. J. Mitchell as *Essay on the True Art of Playing Keyboard Instruments* (London: Eulenberg, 1974).

D'Anglebert, Jean-Henry, 'Principes de l'Accompagnement', in *Pièces de clavecin* (Paris: [author], 1689). Edited by K. Gilbert in *J.-H. D'Anglebert, Pièces de clavecin* (*Le Pupitre*, No. 54), (Paris: Heugel, 1975).

Delair, Denis, *Traité d'Accompagnement pour le Theorbe, et le Clavessin* (Paris: [author], 1690), facsimile reprint (Geneva: Minkoff, 1972). Translated by C. M. Mattax in 'Denis Delair's "Traité d'Accompagnement pour le théorbe, et le clavessin", A translation with commentary', (D.M.A. dissertation, Stanford University, 1985).

Gasparini, Francesco, *L'armonico pratico al cimbalo* (Venice: A. Bortoli, 1708). Translated by F. S. Stillings as *The Practical Harmonist at the Keyboard* (Music Theory Translation Series, 1), (New York: Da Capo, 1980).

Heinichen, Johann David, *Der General-Bass in der Composition* (Dresden: [author], 1728). Partial translation by G. J. Buelow in *Thorough-Bass Accompaniment according to Johann David Heinichen* (Berkeley and Los Angeles: University of California Press, 1966).

Pasquali, Nicolo, *Thorough-Bass Made Easy* (London: Bremner, 1763), facsimile edition by J. Churchill (London: Oxford University Press, 1974).

This is only a tiny selection from a vast field. A very useful annotated 'Handlist of Books' is given by Peter Williams in vol. 1 of his *Figured Bass Accompaniment* (see below).

By far the most useful tutor for the mid- to late Italian baroque style is Gasparini's *L'armonico pratico*, which includes much information on the realization of unfigured basses and on style as well as on basic progressions. A valuable complement to this, though not available in a modern edition, is the *Principi del Sig.*[tr] *Cavaliere Alesandro Scarlatti*, British Library, MS Add. 14244. Pasquali's *Thorough-Bass* has the merit of being an eighteenth-century tutor in English. It also includes realized examples of Italian-style recitative.

Heinichen's *General-Bass* is a very comprehensive expansion of Gasparini's *L'armonico pratico*, and is the fundamental tutor for figured bass practice in Germany. For the late baroque to *galant* style, the second part of C. P. E. Bach's *Versuch* is also very thorough, and contains a great deal more information about style than does Heinichen.

Of the many French tutors, by far the most useful, because it is so concise and practical, is Delair's *Traité*. It should be read in conjunction with D'Anglebert's *Principes*, which gives valuable information about methods of spreading chords and the technique of adding notes to chords. These are a most important part of keyboard performing style both in France and elsewhere. In fact, all D'Angelbert's harpsichord works are much to be recommended, as a means of acquiring an idiomatic harpsichord style, on account of the detailed precision of their notation.

MODERN TUTORS

Arnold, Franck Thomas, *The Art of Accompaniment from a Thorough-Bass* (London: Oxford University Press, 1931; reprinted New York: Dover, 1965).

Keller, Hermann, *Schule des Generalbass-spiels* (Kassel: Bärenreiter, 1931). Translated by C. Parrish as *Thoroughbass Method* (London: Barrie and Rockliff, 1966).

Lemacher, Heinrich, and Schroeder, Hermann, *Generalbassübungen* (third edition, Düsseldorf: Schwann, 1954).

Williams, Peter, *Figured Bass Accompaniment* (Edinburgh: Edinburgh University Press, 1970).

Arnold's monumental *Art of Accompaniment* is likely to remain the starting point for any serious study of figured bass accompaniment. It gives English translations for many of the main sources of information from around 1600 till the late eighteenth century. Williams' *Figured Bass Accompaniment* is particularly useful for assembling information about performing style from a wide variety of sources. Whilst both of these are essential reading for those who have already acquired fluency in playing from figures, neither sets out to be in any way a basic tutor.

For the rudiments of figured bass playing, the most popular and best-designed tutor has been Keller's *Schule*. This gives clear and practical instruction for the ordinary chords and progressions, with well-designed exercises and a selection of graded repertoire for practice. Similar in intent and organization are the *Generalbassübungen* of Lemacher and Schroeder, which use for beginners' exercises the *Gründliche Unterricht des Generalbasses* (1738) attributed to J. S. Bach, and include a number of fugues.

APPENDIX: SPECIMEN REALIZATIONS

Exercises in Figured Bass

No. 1

Play also starting with the third and fifth on top of the first chord.

No. 2

No. 3

No. 4

No. 5

No. 6

No. 7

No. 8

No. 9

No. 10

Decorated version of bb. 11–15. The top part sets off the suspension by falling to the fifth of the 4 chord.

No. 11

No. 12

No. 13

No. 14

No. 15

No. 16

No. 17

No. 18

No. 19

No. 20

No. 21

No. 22

No. 23

No. 24

Exercises in Fugue

No. 1

No. 2

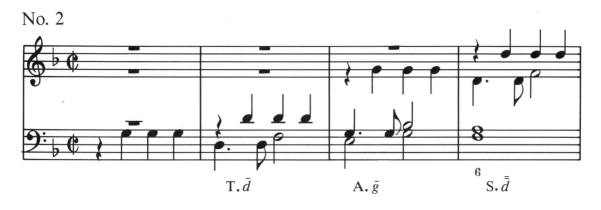

No. 3

No. 4

No. 5

No. 6

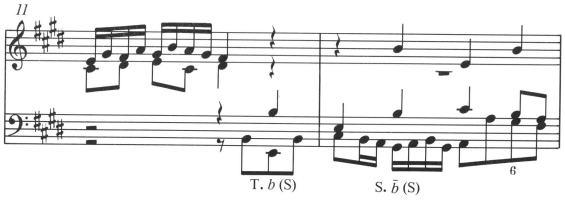

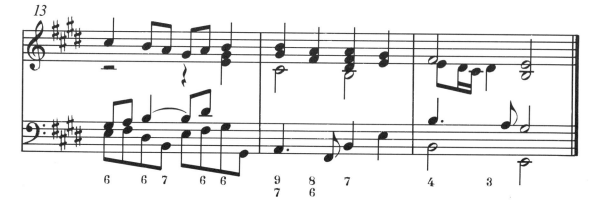